HORRIBLE HISTORIES

EDINBURGH

TERRY DEARY

Illustrated by Mike Phillips

SCHOLASTIC

For Calum March – top Scottish fan.

Scholastic Children's Books,
Euston House, 24 Eversholt Street,
London, NW1 1DB, UK

A division of Scholastic Ltd
London ~ New York ~ Toronto ~ Sydney ~ Auckland
Mexico City ~ New Delhi ~ Hong Kong

First published in the UK by Scholastic Ltd, 2005

10 digit ISBN 0439 95397 9
13 digit ISBN 978 0439 95397 9

Typeset by M Rules
Printed by Nørhaven Paperback A/S, Denmark

2 4 6 8 10 9 7 5 3

The right of Terry Deary and Mike Phillips to be identified as
the author and illustrator of this work respectively has been asserted by
them in accordance with the Copyright, Designs and Patents Act, 1988.

CONTENTS

INTRODUCTION

Edinburgh. Capital city of Scotland. In the 1700s they stuck up some new buildings that looked a bit Greek. Someone said…

EDINBURGH IS THE ATHENS OF THE NORTH

AYE, IT'S FULL OF OLD RUINS LIKE ME!

Edinburgh looks great to the terrible tourists who flock like locusts to see its sights. But they don't always know the dark secrets of its painful past. No one tells them about the human horrors that went on in (and above and below) its savage streets.

What they need is a horrible history of the city. What they need isn't a guide book – it's a gore book. This is it.

I suppose we could start around 355 million years ago when a volcano erupted to make the hill called Arthur's Seat. At that time sharks, water scorpions and fish with armoured heads were swimming around.

Or 205 million years ago when a tourist to Edinburgh would be dodging dinosaurs.

GEE, YOU SCOTS SURE HAVE A WEIRD IDEA OF WELCOMING TOURISTS!

Or 7000 BC when the first humans marched in to massacre the mammoth, butcher the bison and rip up the reindeer.

Or 3000 BC when humans began to settle down. It didn't do them much good. Most of them were dead before they were 30 – and their corpses were left to rot before the bones were buried.

No, let's start at the Bronze Age (about 2000 BC) when people settled on the high rock where Edinburgh Castle stands today. It's hard living on a rock but at least they had some lovely views – they could see when their enemies were coming to get them!

EVIL EDINBURGH TIMELINE

AD **600** A Celtic tribe called the Gododdin moves into the Edinburgh area. But that isn't good enough. No, the men of Gododdin have to go and attack the English at Catterick in Yorkshire. They are wiped out. Big mistake. The English carry out a revenge attack and capture the Gododdin capital Dun Edin. They change its name to the Saxon Edin-burgh.

AD **685** The Anglo-Saxon King Ecgfrid leaves the safety of Edinburgh to attack the Picts in the north. Massive mistake. Ecgfrid and his army are wiped out at Nechtansmere. Ravens peck out the eyes of the Saxon dead. The Saxons won't be back – would you, if your mate had had his eyes pecked out?

AD **844** The Pict tribes from the north join with the Scots tribes (from Ireland). The Pict leader Kenneth MacAlpin becomes king of the Scots. Which town does he choose for his capital?

1076 King Malcolm 'Canmore' ('with the large head') builds a little church for his wife Margaret on the top of the Castle rock. A castle is probably there too. The church is

still there today – the oldest building in Edinburgh. Malc isn't there. He was killed in battle in 1093 trying to conquer England for the fifth time. Margaret dies of a broken heart when she gets the news.

1125 King David I moves his capital from Dunfermline to Edinburgh and makes it a 'royal' town – which means the people have to pay taxes. (They still do!) He is out hunting one day when a stag attacks him. But then a cross magically appears in his hand and drives off the evil creature. He is saved! A cross is also known as a 'rood' – so Dave builds a Holy 'rood' Abbey to say thanks to God. The Palace of Holyroodhouse is there now.

1296 Edward I of England attacks Scotland and captures Edinburgh Castle. English rule OK? (Or not-so-OK if you are a Scot.)

1314 With a small band of men Thomas Randolph, the Earl of Murray, climbs the north face of the rock while the rest of his army attack the south gate. Randolph and his men enter the castle, open the gate and capture the castle from the careless English. They knock a lot of it down.

1328 Robert the Bruce wins back Scotland for the Scots and signs the Treaty of Edinburgh (also signed by Edward III) – which says Rob is king and Scotland is free. Good news? Not really. Rob dies soon after. Bad news for the Scots – lots of weak kings, babies on the throne and bullying English will bring hundreds of years of bloody battles to Edinburgh.

1356 The castle is rebuilt as a palace as well as a fortress.

1456 The Scots build a wall around Edinburgh. The problem is, no one wants to live outside the wall. So they crowd into this part they now call the Old Town. Soon the only way to go is up. Edinburgh has some pretty tall and rickety buildings.

1513 James IV attacks Henry VIII's English troops and loses at Flodden. The Scots worry that Henry will come up to Edinburgh and punish them. They quickly build the Flodden Wall around the city – and bits of their ruins remain today.

1544 Henry's armies get in anyway and burn bits of the town. The Scots invite a French army to protect them.

1559 John Knox becomes minister at the Kirk (Church) of St Giles. He is trouble. His religion is Calvinism –

BUT GOOD NEWS FOR *HORRIBLE HISTORIES* READERS...

I THINK I'M 'EDIN' DOWN!

BLOKES WHO KISS YOU? HELLO! HELLO!

BLOKES IN SKIRTS? OO-LA-LA!

where even good people can burn in hell when they die! He makes enemies with the Catholics, so the Catholic French soldiers are thrown out – even though they were there to help against the English.

1568 Mary Queen of Scots (Catholic) argues with half of the nation – John Knox and his friends. The keeper of Edinburgh Castle, Sir William Kirkcaldy, is on her side and shuts her enemies out. They can't break in because he has all the best guns inside.

1573 The English lend the attackers some cannon. Kirkcaldy is blasted out and executed. The castle is restored the way it looks today.

1603 King James VI takes the English throne peacefully and moves to London. He won't ever come back to rule from Edinburgh. The Scottish will be ruled from England from now on. As James says…

1649 The Scots were fighting with English general Oliver Cromwell to defeat King Charles and give him the chop. Now they switch to fight *against* him. Cromwell beats the Scots at the Battle of Dunbar, marches into Edinburgh and destroys a few churches.

His Roundhead soldiers also wreck the High School.

1707 A new law called 'the Act of Union' joins England and Scotland. Parliament moves to London. The Scottish crown, sword and sceptre are stuffed in a box and locked away. (Amazingly they are found over 100 years later and are still on show.) Not all the Scots like the idea of being joined to England. There are riots.

1736 The Porteous Riots erupt in Edinburgh. A mob of men hang British army captain Porteous. The captain's crime? Hanging a popular smuggler, then killing some of the spectators who threw stones and mud at the executioner.

1745 The last big attack on Edinburgh Castle. Scottish rebel leader Bonnie Prince Charlie snatches Edinburgh from the English though he fails to take the castle.

1767 Edinburgh is crowded – 80,000 people are crammed into the medieval Old Town. So there is a competition to design a new Edinburgh to the north of the castle. Queen Street, Princes Street and George Street form the heart of the New Town.

1822 George IV arrives in Edinburgh – the first British king in Scotland for almost 200 years. The writer Sir Walter Scott prepares a spectacular pageant for the King and dresses the characters in tartan kilts. Suddenly tartan becomes cool – and Edinburgh is the place for terrible tourists to go to.

1824 The Great Fire of Edinburgh. The two-day blaze clears out a lot of rickety slums in the Old Town, so that's all right. Thirteen people are kilt.

1842 The steam railway reaches Edinburgh. The city gets the nickname Auld Reekie – which means Old Smelly. Cough, splutter.

1890 The Forth Bridge opens and lets those tourists get to the Highlands – stopping off at Edinburgh on the way of course.

THE CRUEL CASTLE

Edinburgh Castle sits on its steep rock and scowls down on the city. Just be glad the blood from the castle cruelties dried up long ago, or you'd be swimming in it. Here are a few of the terrible but true stories…

Randolph's ruthless raid

One moonless night in 1314, Thomas Randolph carried out one of the most amazing raids in history. With just 30 men he took the mighty Edinburgh fortress. If newspapers had existed in those days then his daring deed would have hit the headlines like a stone dropped from Edinburgh Castle walls!

1314   **1 Groat**

The Edinburgh Chronicle

CAPTURE THAT CASTLE!

Edinburgh Castle is back in the hands of the Scots after a daring raid that routed the evil English. Last night the brave young Thomas Randolph did the impossible – he climbed the north cliff below the castle. With the help of his top team he placed ladders against the wall, led the way over and massacred the dozy defenders in their beds.

Tom Randolph is of course the nephew of our great leader, Robert the Bruce. Today he opened the castle gates to the *Edinburgh Chronicle* and told us the terrifying tale as the Scots mopped the blood from the cobbles.

TOM, A CHOP OFF THE OLD BLOCK!

First, we asked, why did no one think of this before? Young Thomas laughed. 'Well,' he said, 'we looked at the cliff and didn't think we could do it. Then, last week an old bloke came to me and told me about a path he used to use as a boy. It seems this William Frank chap was a castle guard many years ago. He had a girlfriend who lived in the town and he had to sneak in to see her via a secret route. So he showed us the path, and we made ladders to climb the walls at the top – they're low there because the defenders think it's safe!'

But the attack had a few scary moments. 'A guard looked over the wall just as we reached the top of the cliff. He shouted out, "I can see you!" and threw down a rock. If he'd hit us, or if we'd made a noise, then we would have been dead men. A shower of stones from the guards would have sent us flying down the cliff – and we didn't have wings to save us! Hah! What a scare!'

But it seems the guard was just having a laugh, trying to frighten his mates inside, and had seen nothing. 'It frightened our lads,' Thomas chuckled. 'Old Frank nearly wet himself! But, fair play, the old guy led the way up the ladders. We followed, and Bob's your uncle. Well, Bob IS my uncle, Uncle Bob the Bruce, but I mean Bob's your uncle … if you see what I mean.'

And Uncle Robert the Bruce said today, 'If Edinburgh Castle is so weak, we may as well pull it down and build it again.

But we'll start that tomorrow. Tonight we'll be having a bit of a party to celebrate. Edinburgh Castle is back where it belongs – in true Scottish hands!'

Some of the defenders jumped off the walls to escape the Scottish swords. Don't try this yourself. You may land on someone and hurt them.

GEE, THEY TOLD ME THE *FLYING SCOTSMAN* WAS A TRAIN!

Randolph the ruthless

Thomas Randolph led an odd life before his daring deed at Edinburgh...

- He fought for his Uncle Robert the Bruce but was captured. To save his neck he agreed to fight for the English AGAINST his friends and family.
- While fighting for the English he chased his Uncle Robert with bloodhounds and nearly killed him.
- Then he was captured by his old pals the Scots. Uncle Robert threw him in a dungeon to teach him a lesson.

When Randolph was released, he not only went on to capture Edinburgh Castle but helped beat the English at the Battle of Bannockburn in 1314. The battle set Scotland free – for a while.

Randolph became such a great leader the English couldn't defeat him. He died suddenly in 1332 and the Scots believed the English had had him poisoned!

Heads you lose

There are more ways to capture Edinburgh Castle than struggling to climb its walls. In 1341 the Scottish rebel Sir William Douglas and his men pretended to be merchants. When the castle gates were opened, they stormed in and lopped off the guards' heads. Their bodies were thrown over the castle walls. Don't worry, the long drop didn't hurt one little bit.

Another way to kill your enemies is to invite them to dinner…

The Black Dinner – 29 November 1440

Flaming torches crackled and sizzled on the walls of the castle hall. Young King James II was happy. The nine-year-old boy laughed at his cheerful chief guest, the Earl of Douglas. The Earl was a powerful young man of 16 years; clever and cruel. His younger brother sat beside him and the three boys laughed the way boys do. King James laughed most of all. But then he didn't know what was going to happen. He didn't know he was going to see his first murder.

The meal ended and the plates were cleared away by scurrying servants. Suddenly the door crashed open and the castle guard rushed in. Prince James's mouth fell open as he stared into the dark doorway. Sir William Crichton, keeper of the castle, marched in with a huge silver serving dish. The dish dripped blood because it held the head of a black bull.

'What's this?' King James squeaked.

Sir William ignored him and placed the dish on the table in front of the young Earl of Douglas and his little brother.

'What's this?' echoed the Earl of Douglas.

For a moment Sir William looked confused. 'Don't you know?' he asked.

'I know it's a bull's head,' the Earl sneered. 'What does it mean?'

'Everybody knows what it means!' Sir William snapped.

'I don't,' the Earl said.

'And I don't,' King James piped in.

The guards moved closer to the Earl's shoulder. As he tried to rise to his feet, they pushed him down. 'It is a sign that a death sentence has been passed on you.'

'On me?'

'Your enemies are tired of your troublesome ways. They got me to invite you here tonight to execute you.'

The Earl struggled to pull a dagger from his belt. Strong hands stopped him.

'You can't do that, Sir William!' King James cried. 'I forbid it. I am King and I forbid it.'

The keeper of the castle shrugged. 'Sorry, Your Majesty, but the Scottish lords have ordered this execution and even you cannot stop it.'

'Execution?' The Earl of Douglas laughed bitterly. 'Murder, more like.'

'Spare them!' King James wailed, but the brothers were tied with ropes and dragged from the hall. The King ran to the window and watched. A single torch guttered in the cold November night as two young heads were struck from their bodies.

Edinburgh Castle was cursed for its part in the cruel deed. A minstrel sang that he hoped it would sink into the ground. The old verse is still remembered today...

Edinburgh Castle, town and tower, God grant that you sink for your sin.

The murder became known as 'The Black Dinner'. It must have upset James II's young brain and turned him vicious. Twelve years later he was having dinner at Stirling Castle with the new Earl of Douglas. Suddenly James II drew his knife and stabbed his guest. The Earl didn't die – at least not until the servants finished him off for their King. They beat his brains out.

James II died when he attacked Roxburgh Castle. One of his own cannon exploded and blew off his leg.

The long siege

Mary Queen of Scots inherited the throne as a little girl in 1542 but by 1568 she had to run away to England (find out why on page 70).

Brave Sir William Kirkcaldy of Grange was the governor of Edinburgh Castle. He promised to look after the castle for Mary and keep out her enemies until she could come back with an army.

But Sir William's enemies kept him trapped inside for two years, from 1571 till 1573. Then they borrowed huge English guns from Berwick to batter him out. The diary of death was about to begin…

25 APRIL 1573

A TRUMPETER CALLED TO SIR WILLIAM IN THE CASTLE...

SURRENDER OR WE FIRE!

RAISE A RED FLAG TO SHOW WE WILL NEVER SURRENDER!

15 MAY 1573

THIRTY GUNS WERE AIMED AT THE CASTLE. TWO OF THEM COULD FIRE 45 kg (100 lb) CANNONBALLS

WE HAVE TO USE A CRANE TO LOAD THE THINGS!

17 MAY 1573

ALL THE GUNS OPENED FIRE TOGETHER. THE CASTLE GUNS FIRED BACK. IN BREAKS BETWEEN FIRE SCREAMS COULD BE HEARD FROM WOMEN IN THE CASTLE

AIEEE! THEY'LL DIRTY ME WASHING!

THEY'LL CANNON ME KILT!

23 MAY 1573

AT LAST DAVID'S TOWER, ALONG WITH ITS GUNS AND MEN, TUMBLED DOWN THE CLIFFS TO THEIR DOOM

THANKS FOR DROPPING IN TO SEE US!

28 MAY 1573

THE ATTACKERS CAPTURED THE MAIN WELL AND POISONED ANOTHER WELL. SIR WILLIAM WAS LOWERED OVER THE WALL IN HIS ARMOUR

I WANT PEACE TALKS

I DON'T. I WANT YOUR COMPLETE SURRENDER OR NOTHING

29 MAY 1573

THE 100 DEFEATED DEFENDERS MARCHED OUT PROUDLY WITH THEIR WIVES AND CHILDREN, BANNERS FLYING

THANK GOODNESS. THOSE CANNON GAVE ME A HEADACHE

30 MAY 1573

BUT THERE WAS NO HAPPY ENDING FOR POOR SIR WILLIAM. HE WAS DRAGGED ON A SLEDGE TO THE MERCAT CROSS AND HANGED ALONG WITH HIS BROTHER

POOR MAN. I'M CHOKED WITH EMOTION

BUT NOT AS CHOKED AS THE KIRKCALDY BROTHERS!

1 JUNE 1573

THEIR HEADS WERE HACKED OFF AND STUCK ON THE RUINED CASTLE WALLS

I SPY WITH MY LITTLE EYE SOMETHING BEGINNING WITH 'E'

EDINBURGH?

NO... OUR 'EADLESS CORPSES

Did you know…?
In 1603 Francis Maubray was locked in the castle, awaiting trial. He tried to escape but was killed. His corpse was taken to court anyway. He was found guilty and his body was hanged, beheaded and cut into quarters. Don't worry, it probably didn't hurt.

September slaughter
In September 1745 Bonnie Prince Charlie led an army of rebels from the Highlands. They arrived in Edinburgh, where General Guest, aged 85, was in command of the castle. Charlie's men captured several houses close to the castle and stopped food getting in. The angry General Guest wrote to the Edinburgh Council and said…

My Dear Lord Provost and Council,

I write to warn your people that unless these rebels allow our supplies through, I shall be forced to fire upon them. So there! Of course I don't want any innocent people getting blown up! ✳ General Guest…

But Bonnie Prince Charlie got his hands on the letter and wrote back…

> My Dear General Guest,
> How generally unfair of you to expect the People of Edinburgh to be able to throw us out. You would be wrong to blow them to bits.
>   Prince Charlie

General Guest agreed to hold his fire till he had orders from the King in London. But the next day a supply wagon creaked up the street to the castle. The headstrong Highlanders fired at it. The defenders in the castle fired back and began to blast the houses too. Both Highlanders and innocent people were slaughtered.

The people of Edinburgh thought grumpy old Guest must have been desperate for food supplies. But the people were wrong! The castle had plenty of food. It was all part of Guest's plan…

I WANTED THE REBELS TO STAY IN EDINBURGH, THAT WOULD STOP THEM ATTACKING ENGLAND! I HAVE BRAINS, EH?

I USED TO HAVE BRAINS BEFORE YOU BLEW THEM OUT!

AWFUL OLD TOWN

Edinburgh grew up … and up. Some houses were 14 storeys high – the very first skyscrapers. The smoke from the coal fires made a stinking cloud above the city that could be seen 80 km (50 miles) away. The smell from the crowded houses was ten times worse than a school toilet. And the people could be violent and vile.

THIS IS MY DIRTY, ROTTEN, STINKING, HORRIBLE HOME, FIND YOUR OWN!

THANKS, DAD!

You would NOT want to live in Edinburgh in the putrid past. Look at some of the horrible history…

Foul facts

Sir William Brereton, a commander in Cromwell's army, visited Edinburgh in 1635 and was shocked by what he saw. He was a bit of an English snob. His report was so frightful that we've missed out the disgusting words. Can you replace the numbers with them? (If you are an English snob, you may not want to of course.)

You want a clue? Oh, very well. Here are the missing words in the wrong order. Makes it too easy, but you did ask: *mould, food, nose, toilet, cloth, pee, grease, feet, supper, cup*

Report: Edinburgh 1635

Sir William Brereton

The city has a beautiful air but the people are dirty and lazy. When I walked through the dining room, I had to hold my (1) because of the smell of their clothes, their toilets and their (2).

Your (3) at dinner has never been washed, only rubbed over with a filthy (4) dipped in water full of (5). The wine jugs are covered in (6) and you would not want to drink from them.

The kitchen sink looks like a (7) and it is enough to put you off your (8).

The bedclothes are washed by women's (9). They come out looking as dirty as ours do before we wash them and they smell of (10).

When I got into bed, I had to hold my breath.

Potty laws

It was against the law to empty your toilet pot from the high Edinburgh flats into the road below – someone walking in the street could get very smelly. The English writer Daniel Defoe said that people in the street had to cry out...

HOLD YOUR HAND! DON'T THROW TILL I'M PAST!

In the 1700s people were still emptying their stinky pots but they didn't get caught. Everyone in the flats blamed everyone else and the law didn't know who to blame! Whose poo? Who nose?

Not-so-nice New Town

Edinburgh is also called the 'Venice of the North' – which is even dafter than calling it the 'Athens of the North' because Venice has canals instead of streets. But of course, on a wet day in Edinburgh you *could* be walking through canals. The Edinburgh-born writer Robert Louis Stevenson said...

26

> *Edinburgh can be beaten by all the winds that blow, drenched with rain, buried in cold sea fogs from the East and powdered with snow from the Highland hills. The weather is raw in winter, unfriendly in summer and hellish in spring. The weak children die young. I sometimes think they are the lucky ones.*

Did you know…?

In 1866 a 20-year-old woman in old Edinburgh had an unusual job. She was paid to be sent to prison! She lived in a house full of thieves who robbed drunken men on a Saturday night. The thieves bribed her to save them from the law. If the police found stolen goods in the house then the young woman took the blame and went to prison.

WOE FOR WITCHES

Scotland and witches go together like haggis and bashed swedes[1]. William Shakespeare even wrote a play about a gang of wicked witches who helped murdering Scottish King Macbeth take the throne. But Shakespeare's play was wildly wrong about King Macbeth, who was rather a nice chap and a good king. Other ideas about witches are just as potty – but sadly several thousand suffered because of these idiot ideas. Here are a few true cases...

The tortured traitor

Walter Stewart, Earl of Atholl, met a group of witches who told him he was going to be crowned in Edinburgh. All he had to do was bump off the man on the throne – King James I. Walter caught the King near Perth and assassinated him in 1437. Did he get the crown? Well, no, not exactly. He was arrested and executed v-e-r-y slowly. In fact it took three days. The Queen, Anne, planned it.

> FIRST WE HAUL HIM UP ON A CRANE WITH ROPE TIED AROUND HIS ANKLES. WHEN THE CRANE LETS HIM DROP, HIS JOINTS WILL BE TORN

> BUNGEE-JUMPING IS FUN!

1 Bashed swedes are mashed turnips, not Viking visitors who have been beaten up.

28

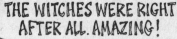

NEXT DAY WE GET A CROWN WITH THE WORDS 'KING OF TRAITORS' ON IT. THEN WE HEAT IT UP AND JAM IT ON HIS HEAD

THE WITCHES WERE RIGHT AFTER ALL. AMAZING!

FIZZ!

ON THE THIRD DAY HIS GUTS AND HIS HEART ARE RIPPED OUT, WHILE HE IS STILL ALIVE, AND THROWN ON THE FIRE

CAN YOU SMELL SAUSAGES?

FINALLY, WE BEHEAD HIM AND CUT HIM INTO QUARTERS. ANYONE ELSE FANCY A TRY AT TREASON?

DEPENDS WITCH WAY YOU WANT TO GO!

The Earl of Atholl's grandson was taken to his execution with his hands nailed to the cart. The executioner stuck red-hot spikes into his legs as they rolled along. Then he was gutted and beheaded.

Witch-killing king

As I said, the Scots had a thing about witches. Down in England they had the odd witch hunt and hanged a few helpless people. But in Scotland they had more terrible tortures and more evil executions ... because in Scotland witches were *burned* alive at the stake.

• In the 1500s and 1600s the Scots burned 4,000 victims.
• The last burning took place in 1722.
• The last witch to be hanged was in 1728.
• In Edinburgh 300 were burned near the castle.
• A well in the east corner of the castle now marks where the stake stood.

There were four big bouts of burnings in Scotland: 1590 to 1597, 1628 to 1630, 1649 and 1661 to 1662. Blame King James VI of Scotland for starting it. He was on his way back to Scotland when his ship was caught in a storm. Unlucky?

Seventy people were arrested. Some said the witchcraft plot was true – though of course they were being tortured at the time. One witch, Old John Cunningham, said...

The top witch was Agnes Samson and she was taken to Holyroodhouse to be tried. King James himself watched the trial. Her case looked something like this...

WHICH WITCH?

First name: *Agnes*

Last name: *Samson*

Sex: *Female*

Home country: *Edinburgh*

Start of trial: *22 November 1590*

End of trial: *8 May 1591*

Offence: *Two attempts to sink royal ships by throwing live cats into the sea at Leith with a dead man's bones and joints tied to them. These made storms on 1 May 1590 that almost killed Queen Anne and King James.*

Trying to kill the king by making wax dolls of him and melting them.

Skills: *Black magic: making corpse powder for spells from dead bodies and grease from the fat of a dead child.*

Talking with devils and fairies.

Changing the weather and making storms.

Causing death and disease in enemies.

White magic: healing, love spells, seeing the future, finding lost things.

Devil's mark:
On her right knee. She said it was where one of her children had kicked her.

Notes: *The devil came to her after her husband died. She plotted for the chance to take revenge on the rich because she was poor. To get healing powers, she called the devil by the name of 'Elva' and he came to her in the shape of a dog. He also appeared as a white stag and a stack of hay.*

She looked into the future and saw someone's death. She confessed to these things in front of king James VI.

Agnes was tortured. First she was made to suffer the Witch's Bridle (a favourite torture of King James). She was pinned to a wall of her cell by an iron mask that had four sharp prongs. These were forced into her mouth, and through her tongue and cheeks.

Then she was 'thawed' – a rope was wrapped around her head and twisted tighter and tighter, crushing her skull.

Then she was kept without sleep for several days.

Finally she was taken to Castle Hill, strangled and burned. King James wrote a book about the problem…

It would have saved a lot of misery if they had just burned James and his book instead.

Did you know…?

Want a recipe for killing someone with black magic? Take some stale pee, mix it with the juices from a crushed toad and feed it to the victim.

Did you also know…?

The deep-fried Mars bar is one of Scotland's greatest inventions. A Mars bar is dipped in batter and dropped into boiling fat. In 2004 more than one in five (22 %) of fish and chip shops across Scotland sold deep-fried Mars bars.

The battered delight seems to have been invented in The Haven chip shop in Stonehaven, north-eastern Scotland. Apparently the shop owner did it for a bet.

There are 400 calories in this tasty treat which is served with chips. Eating too many will make you fat.

Horrible Histories warning:

Scotland has about the highest number of people with heart disease, cancer and strokes, the worst teeth and the shortest lives in Europe. Keep off the deep-fried Mars bars and stick to the stale pee and toad juice!

So now you don't have to burn witches to kill them – just feed them deep-fried Mars bars.

HORRIBLE HIGH STREET

The main street in Edinburgh has seen some of the grisliest and most gruesome sights in the history of Scotland – in fact it could well be the most horribly historical street in the whole world. Take a stroll down this blood-stained street and feel the power of its putrid past...

The terrible Tolbooth prison

The Tolbooth stood on the High Street and around 1590 was filled with poor people accused of witchcraft. But that's not the only savage story about the jolly old jail...

Horrible Histories warning:
Do not read this story if you are about to eat some dinner. Or don't blame me if you throw up.

Sawney Bean
If Sawney Bean said, 'I'd love to have you for tea,' he didn't mean he'd like to *invite* you to tea. He meant he'd like to *eat* you for his tea.

The story goes that this cruel cannibal was born in East Lothian (close to Edinburgh) around the 1200s or 1300s. Sawney hated his farm job in East Lothian so he ran away with his new wife to live in a cave on the beach in Galloway in south-west Scotland.

How did they survive? For 25 years they robbed and murdered travellers. What did they eat? They ate their murder victims, munching their way through about one person a week. If the family couldn't manage a whole man for dinner, they hung up the leftovers in the cave. A smoky fire stopped them going off.

Over the years many innocent people were arrested and executed for the Bean family's crimes. The family were careful never to let anyone escape. But then one evening they leapt out on a husband and wife, who were on horseback. The poor wife was dragged to the ground, her throat was cut and the Beans drank her blood. Just as they were tearing out her bowels, a gang of horsemen arrived and the horrified husband was able to escape. When he returned to the coast he had an army of 400 of the King's men. The Beans were hunted down, arrested and taken to Edinburgh for execution. The King decided not to waste time with a trial. Now we get to the really nasty bit... not thinking about dinner, are you?

Horrible Histories quick question: What did the visitor say as she watched the women and children roast to death? Go on, have a guess. Yes, that's right...

A popular poem of 200 years ago told the Bean family's grim tale…

> They've hung them high in Edinburgh town,
> An' likewise a their kin,
> And the wind blows cold upon their bones,
> And to hell they all have gone.

Now that is as horrible a story as you would never wish to hear. But the good news is that it is just a legend. YES, there were probably robbers on the Galloway coast, BUT the cannibal family that escaped for 25 years is nonsense. And there are no records of the bloody executions in Edinburgh. They were supposed to have happened at the Tolbooth prison, but it wasn't even built then – it was built in 1561.

So it's safe to swim on the Galloway beaches. Sawney Bean will not be seen.

Did you know…?
The Tolbooth prison used to stand in the High Street but was knocked down in 1817. Today the site is marked by a heart-shaped pattern of cobblestones. For luck you are supposed to spit into the heart.

High Street hatred

In April 1520 the people of Glasgow marched across to Edinburgh to take over the government on behalf of their leaders, the Earl of Arran and the Archbishop of Glasgow. This mob was a bit like a gang of angry football supporters today – except its members were armed with swords (whereas today's supporters are armed with meat pies and mobile phones).

The mobsters reached the High Street – the street that runs down from the castle to the town centre. Their Edinburgh enemies, led by the Earl of Angus, blocked the street and stopped the Glasgow gang from getting to the castle. But the Edinburgh men were short of weapons.

What did the people of Edinburgh do? They passed the defenders spears from the windows of their homes and the Glasgow swords were driven back. The Earl of Arran, the Glasgow leader, just managed to escape. How?

a) He was carried off by an Edinburgh knight on a white horse. What a gentleman. (The knight, not the horse.)

b) He caught a coal horse (a horse used to pull coal carts, not a horse made of coal) and rode to safety.

c) He jumped on a sledge and shot down the High Street to freedom. (Did I mention it was snowing?)

Answer: b) The Earl of Arran grabbed a mucky old coal horse and jumped on its back. He pulled his son up behind him and they clopped off, defeated.

40

Haunted High Street

In the early 1800s someone found the entrance to a secret passage leading from the castle. It was so narrow that no man could climb down, so the council sent a little drummer boy along the underground tunnel instead.

The wee boy rattled his drum as he crept along, and the council kept their ears to the ground, following the sound down the High Street. But when it reached the Tron Church the drumming stopped. It never started again and the boy never reappeared. The council sealed up the entrance and it hasn't been found since.

On quiet nights, they say, you can still hear a faint drumming coming from under the High Street! Believe that … if you want to.

MISERABLE MERCAT CROSS

Of course not all of ancient Edinburgh's horrors happened in the castle. The streets saw their share of blood and fire too. It seems every corner and square in the Old Town has a tale of terror...

Cries of a cursed king

The army of James IV was cursed. In 1513 they planned to invade England. But on the night before the army set off from Edinburgh there was a terrible cry heard at the Mercat Cross – the Scots name for the Edinburgh market place.

THE FOLLOWING MEN ARE DOOMED TO DIE... LISTEN VERY CAREFULLY, YOU KILTED CLOWNS, FIRST, KING JAMES...

A loud voice wailed out the names of the lords and knights who would die in the war. No one knew if the voice was a human's or a spirit's ... but the legend says that the men who were named never came back alive. A man called Richard Lawson said he saw the cursing crier and claimed it was the devil himself.

Some people think this REALLY happened, but it wasn't a ghost and it wasn't the devil. It was all set up by James IV's wife, Queen Margaret. Why would the quaint Queen do such a queer thing? To stop her husband going off to war. Alas, poor James was killed anyway – at the Battle of Flodden Field.

Spooky or what? Be very careful if you hear a voice in the dark calling out YOUR name.

Dying to entertain you

If you wanted to witness a horrid hanging or an exciting execution then Edinburgh was the place to be. All you had to do was head for the miserable Mercat Cross on Edinburgh's Royal Mile and you would witness the worried victims being hurried to their death…

NAH! WE MAKE A PARADE OUT OF IT. HAVE A FEW SPEECHES, EVEN LET THE VICTIM SPEAK – SELL LOTS OF PIES AND BEERS... THE PEOPLE NEED A HOLIDAY

SO WHERE DO WE HAVE THIS EXECUTION?

WE'LL NEED A BIT OF SPACE TO GET ALL THE CROWDS IN. HOW ABOUT THE BIGGEST SQUARE IN EDINBURGH – THE SQUARE WHERE THEY HOLD THE MARKET

THE MERCAT SQUARE?

THAT'S THE ONE. A GREAT PLACE FOR A PUBLIC EXECUTION. LET'S DO IT!

John Dickson

In July 1588 young Dickson killed his father. He was taken to the Mercat Cross for a hideous punishment – breaking on the rack. First he was tied to a frame by his wrists and ankles, and his bones were broken with an iron bar. Then he was left there all night to die slowly before his body was carried off to be put on show. It was a lesson to all young men: 'Don't do away with your dad.'

SO THAT'S WHY THEY SAY 'RACKED' WITH PAIN!

Miserable Montrose

One of the most famous executions was that of James Graham, the Marquis of Montrose, in 1650. At the time, Scotland was ruled by the 'Covenanters', who believed God was more important than the King. Montrose invaded to win Scotland for King Charles I. But he was defeated at the Battle of Philiphaugh near the border. For five years he tried to raise an army and carry on the fight but was finally captured. The Covenanters sentenced him to death. Montrose was happy to hear it. He said…

MY KING, CHARLES I, WAS BEHEADED. I HAVE JOY IN MY HEART. I WILL DIE THE SAME WAY AND I WILL DIE FOR HIM

Montrose was taken back to Edinburgh to hang – and he was lucky! A preacher said…

GOD WANTS THE BLOOD OF ALL THE ENEMY PRISONERS WE CAPTURED AT PHILIPHAUGH!

The prisoners were shot or just thrown over a bridge into the Ettrick River. A lord was usually executed with an axe – but the Covenanters were feeling spiteful and they sentenced Montrose to hang like a common thief. On 21 May 1650, Montrose was tied to a chair and placed in a cart that was driven through the streets to the Mercat Cross.

- He was wearing a new suit made for the execution – a lace coat, scarlet cloak and red silk stockings.
- He had to climb a ladder over nine metres high at the top of which a rope was placed round his neck.
- The ladder was taken away and he was left to swing for three hours.
- One of Montrose's laws was hung round his neck to be mocked at along with the corpse.
- Montrose was cut down and his body carved up.
- His head was stuck on Edinburgh Tolbooth (where people coming into Edinburgh would see it).
- His arms and legs were sent to Glasgow, Stirling, Perth and Aberdeen to be put on show.
- His body was buried in a common grave – but his wife dug it up and had the heart mummified. It was sent to his son in Holland.

When King Charles II came to the throne ten years later, Montrose's body was put back together and he was given a proper funeral at Holyrood Abbey in Edinburgh. Stories say his heart was taken by sea to India, stolen by an Indian prince, then brought back to Europe by land. It vanished in Paris during the French Revolution around 150 years later.

HE'S A MAN AFTER MY OWN HEART

Montrose was a bit of a show-off. In February 1638 he had a scaffold built so that he could read out one of his laws to the people. But the scaffold wasn't high enough for him so he stood on a barrel. His friend the Duke of Rothes said…

Jamie, you will not be happy till you be lifted up there nine yards on the end of a rope.

Little did he know!

And another thing…
Montrose's grey ghost now haunts the ruins of Ardvreck Castle, where he may have been held before being sent to his execution. Maybe he's looking for revenge… or maybe he's looking for the heart his wife nicked!

The Earl of Argyll
The ninth Earl of Argyll, Archibald Campbell, was executed at the Mercat Cross in 1685 and, it has to be said, it served him right. In 1681 it was Charles's turn to execute the Covenanters and Archibald of Argyll was sent to Edinburgh Castle for the chop. But artful Archie managed to escape! How? Did he…

a) disguise himself as something else and walk out?

b) jump off the walls with a parachute?

c) dip himself in invisible ink and escape from his pen?

Only joking. He didn't dress as a page from a book – he dressed as a *page*... You know, a page boy.

Anyway, it worked. Argyll fled to Holland, where he was safe. Then there was a rebellion against King James VII and Argyll came back to fight. Of course the King won, Argyll was captured and sentenced to death a SECOND time. Some people never learn, do they? Archibald of Argyle was beheaded at the Mercat Cross and died with a smile on his face because he thought he was going straight to heaven. He said...

I am happier today than I was the day I escaped from the castle.

Happy? He must have been laughing his head off.

Maggie Dickson

Maggie Dickson killed a child and so, on 2 September 1724, she was hanged in Edinburgh. The doctor signed the death certificate to say she was stone dead and her body was placed in a casket, put on a cart and taken off to the graveyard. But, on the way Maggie sat up – and scared the life out of the cart driver.

IS THIS HEAVEN?

OH, HELL!

The town council decided it couldn't hang her again, as you can't hang a dead person. So Meg was allowed to live and she went on to marry and have a family. She died 30 years later and was known ever after as Half Hangit Maggie.

REVOLTING RIOTS

The people of Edinburgh could be stroppy at times. Something upset them and off they went on a riot. It was a bit of fun … unless you were one of the victims, of course.

Wilson the smuggler

Smugglers used to bring booze into Edinburgh. They didn't pay taxes to the government so it was cheap. The people liked that. The government didn't. In 1736 the army started catching, arresting and executing smugglers. The people didn't like that. It led to trouble. As an army report might have said…

Edinburgh, March 1736

Andrew Wilson was taken from his cell in chains at 2 p.m. I have been asked to write this report of what I saw at the Wilson execution.

Wilson had already tried to escape. His partner Robertson got away when the two men were taken to church last Sunday. Wilson started fighting the guards while Robertson made a run for it. The common people believe Wilson is a bit of a hero.

A large crowd had gathered at the Grassmarket and so Captain Porteous ordered an armed guard to escort the prisoner. The executioner managed to hang Wilson. But before he could cut down the corpse, the bad-tempered mob began to throw stones and mud at him. They did not make a rush to snatch the corpse and carry it off for a burial. They did not try to attack the guards.

Still, Captain Porteous gave the order for the soldiers to fire.

I believe that Captain Porteous had drunk a lot of wine with his dinner. His face was red and angry. He meant his guards to kill. Most of the soldiers fired over the heads of the crowd. Sadly, there were people sitting in the windows of the houses and one lad was killed.

Porteous ordered the soldiers to aim at the crowd and another eight died. Many more were wounded.

Porteous the soldier

The people of Edinburgh were shocked. They said that Porteous should be arrested for murder. He was, and was found guilty and sentenced to death. The Edinburgh folk were happy with that and looked forward to the execution of the pompous Porteous. Then news came of a royal letter…

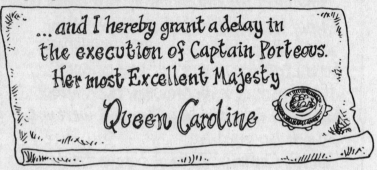

... and I hereby grant a delay in the execution of Captain Porteous. Her most Excellent Majesty

Queen Caroline

Porteous was NOT set free and was still sentenced to hang. But the hanging had been put off by the Queen. Everyone was furious. They decided the law was too weak. They would take their own revenge.

Edinburgh, 7 September 1736

Report on the hanging of Captain Porteous

I was on guard at the Tolbooth prison, on the night of 7 September, when I heard hammering at the main gate. The guards said it was a mob come to hang Captain Porteous.

The gates were smashed and a gang of men in disguise rushed for the prison cells.

Captain Porteous had thrown off his clothes so he could climb up the chimney to safety. But he was dragged back down and dressed in his nightshirt. The mobsters hauled him through the streets and no one tried to stop them. They took him to the Grassmarket, where Andrew Wilson had been hanged. There was no time to build a gallows so they threw the rope over a barber's pole outside a shop. The rioters hauled him up, kicking and struggling, and struck at him with their pikes and swords till he was dead.

The scene was lit with smoking torches but I could not make out the faces of the killers. They were hidden behind masks. When the savage crowd had gone, we went up and cut down our Captain Porteous.

He was dead.

The government never discovered who killed Captain Porteous, though it is said there were some important Edinburgh men in the mob. No one felt sorry for Porteous. No one wept for his horrible hanging.

Bad boys

In 1595 the boys of Edinburgh High School staged a riot to demand more holidays. They barricaded themselves in a classroom in the school. The town bailie (top cop) went to sort them out. One of the boys had a pistol and shot the bailie clean between the eyes. The boys gave up their protest.

What happened next?

a) The boy who shot the bailie was hanged.

b) All the boys in the school were whipped 20 times and set free.

c) The headmaster was sacked and the teachers had their pay cut.

Answer: c) The boys went free. The teachers were blamed for the riot and the head was sacked — which serves him right for being called Hercules Rollocks.

I STILL THINK THEY SHOULD HAVE SACKED ALL THE TEACHERS

CREEPY CHURCHES

The Edinburgh mob didn't just riot over a hanging. They rioted over some words printed on a page – rather as you would if your school printed 'Punishment for breathing in class: half an hour's detention.' Words can be very annoying things.

Prayer-book riot

The Covenanters refused to have King Charles I's Book of Common Prayer in their churches. They went to Greyfriars Church in Edinburgh, where they signed a letter to say they all refused. Many were so angry that they signed the letter in their own blood.

- They lost the Battle of Bothwell Bridge in 1679 and paid for it.
- 1,200 beaten Covenanters were kept for five months without shelter in a corner of Greyfriars churchyard.
- The only food each man got was a handful of water and a penny loaf (about 120 g) every day.
- If they tried to get up during the night, the guards would shoot them.
- They were sent to the West Indies to work as slaves, but the ship was wrecked near the Orkney Islands and only 40 survived.

Jenny of St Giles

In 1637 there was a protest against Catholic ways in St Giles' Cathedral. The famous Edinburgh story goes like this…

THE DEAN OF ST GILES BEGAN TO READ FROM KING CHARLES I'S NEW PRAYER BOOK

LET US PRAY…

BUT THE PROTESTANTS THOUGHT IT SOUNDED TOO MUCH LIKE THE CATHOLIC SERVICE…

MUTTER! MUTTER!

A WOMAN CALLED JENNY GEDDES STOOD UP AND CRIED…

HOW DARE YOU FILL MY LUGS WITH THAT CATHOLIC STUFF!

THEN SHE PICKED UP A STOOL AND THREW IT AT THE BISHOP

TAKE THAT!

YOU TELL HIM!

BUT … this famous 'true' tale of a brave Scotswoman may not be so true after all. It may be just a legend. The only report written at the time said a mob shouted at the bishop and pelted him with stones…

I THINK I LIKE THE STOOL STORY BETTER!

Chop that church

In 1688 King James VII of Scotland (and II of England) turned Catholic. You'd think he'd have more sense!

HOW MANY TIMES DO I HAVE TO SAY THIS? I DO NOT LIKE CATHOLICS IN SCOTLAND!

AND I'M RIGHT BEHIND HIM!

The Catholic religion liked fine churches full of paintings and extra statues and seats that were cleverly carved. The Protestants liked plain churches. King Dim Jim decided to turn the Protestant abbey church at Holyrood into a Catholic church. The Scottish judge Sir John Lauder said…

> *So this was the first Protestant church taken away from us. It was also the last.*

A Protestant king, William of Orange, threw out King Dim Jim so the Scots could have their church back! William marched on Edinburgh. Sir Daniel Wilson of Edinburgh described what happened next...

> *The Catholic Earl of Perth left Edinburgh very quickly. That was a sign for the mob to attack the abbey church. James's troop of 100 men defended it with guns, which they fired into the mob. They killed 12 and wounded many more. But this just made the mob angrier. In the end they defeated the soldiers and entered the church. The fine carved seats (just finished) were turned into ruins. The rioters wrecked the church then marched up to the Mercat Cross, where they had a bonfire and burned a dummy of the Pope.*

They also ripped up the coffins of the kings who were buried there and the bones were scattered around. James had to run away to France. The Edinburgh mob had won again.

Groovy graveyards

As you would expect, some of Edinburgh's creepiest events took place in its graveyards. And the city has some spooky stories to tell.

The most famous corpse in Greyfriars churchyard is the little dog Greyfriars Bobby. There is a statue of the dog outside the grounds and a film was made of his sad tail … er, I mean *tale*. His master, a farmer named John Gray, died one market day in 1858 and was buried in the churchyard. For 14 years the loyal little dog refused to leave his graveside, even in bad weather, and the local people fed Bobby for 14 years till he died. What they never tell you is Bobby could not be buried in holy ground because he was a dog. They stuck his poor canine corpse outside the graveyard.

Did you know…?

Greyfriars graveyard is haunted, but not by a doggy demon. George Mackenzie (1636–1691) was a judge during King Charles II's reign. His violent torturing and killing of the Covenanter rebels got him the nickname Bloody Mackenzie. He is buried in a large black tomb in Greyfriars graveyard. The story goes that his wicked spirit cannot rest – God won't let him into heaven! – so he wanders round his tomb each night. Visitors have reported being attacked. They have bruises and scratches to prove it. Some have even been knocked out.

Here's a nice Hallowe'en game for you. Children used to dare each other to knock on the door of his tomb and yell at him. The trick was to run away before the corpse rose from its coffin and caught you.

Horrible Histories note: Do not try this with your granny – especially if she is still alive.

TERRIBLE TRUTHS

Here is a simple test – that is a test for simple people. All you have to do is…
1 Answer 'true' or 'false'.
2 Get it right.
Simple? Then off you go.

1 In Edinburgh in 1865 Dr William Pritchard murdered his mother-in-law with a sausage.

2 In 1864 George Bryce was the last man to be hanged in public in Edinburgh. Over 20,000 people turned up to watch him die. It was the largest crowd in Edinburgh since a relative of Bryce's was hanged 20 years before.

IT'S NICE TO KEEP THE FAMILY TRADITIONS GOING

3 In the 1700s Edinburgh fishermen could not go to sea in the winter storms. Their wives sold cute little larks to eat instead.

4 In 1770 Edinburgh was attacked by the American navy.

5 In 1888 a group of Edinburgh boys played football with a paper parcel. The parcel burst open and there was a dead haggis inside.

6 Some Edinburgh chimney sweeps tied children to a rope and pulled them up and down a chimney to clean it.

7 The famous Protestant preacher John Knox is buried under a car park in Parliament Square.

8 In 1707 the Earl of Drumlanrig ate a kitchen boy.

9 In Greyfriars churchyard a gang of bodysnatchers dug up an old woman's coffin. They found she was still alive.

10 Ebenezer Scrooge, the famous miser in Charles Dickens's book *A Christmas Carol*, is buried in Edinburgh.

Answers:

1 True. He fed her a poisoned sausage and she died. When that worked he fed his wife poison and she died too. He was hanged in Glasgow.

2 True. Bryce had murdered his girlfriend. In Edinburgh's Royal Mile you will find a brass letter H set in the pavement. That is the spot where the hanging took place. Have a quick look – but don't hang about.

3 True. They caught them in nets. These birds are very tasty if you eat them roasted.

GO ON, TRY IT, JUST FOR A LARK!

Bird lovers were shocked and stopped the trade. The larks lived – the fishermen went hungry.

4 True. John Paul Jones was a Scot but he went to America to build the country's navy. Britain went to war with America and Jones sailed home – to blast Edinburgh with the cannon on his warship. An old priest watched from the shore and said...

God could easily send a wind to blow them away.

What happened next? A storm blew up and drove the American ships away! People said it was a miracle. Maybe God is a Scot after all.

5 False. It was much worse than that. There was a dead baby inside, aged about one year. The baby's father had given the baby to Jessie King to look after. He paid the woman five pounds. Mrs King was one of those Victorian villains...

A BABY FARMER?

The baby farmers took the parents' money and promised to look after the child. If the child died quickly then the baby farmer made a good profit. If the baby DIDN'T die 'naturally' then the baby farmers sometimes helped it to die.

Jessie King gave the baby whisky to keep it quiet and she said the whisky killed the child by accident. But the doctor said it was strangled. Jessie King was hanged – the last woman to be hanged in Edinburgh.

6 True. The cruellest sweeps took children on to the rooftops. They tied ropes to the children's arms and legs, dropped them down the chimney, then hauled them back up again. This meant the scruffy children didn't trample over the nice carpets in the rich people's homes. The children didn't do much brushing – their little bodies WERE the brushes. The sweeps who used this method were taken to court and punished.

If a little sweep got stuck then a second child could be sent up with a lighted match to burn his feet and make him wriggle free.

7 False … probably. Go to Parliament Square and you will see a small yellow square in parking space number 44. It SAYS John Knox is buried there – and he probably WAS at one time. But the graveyard and the bodies were moved. No rest for the wicked, they say.

John Marlin was a Frenchman who, in 1532, had the job of covering the High Street in paving stones. He was so proud of his work that he asked to be buried underneath the road when he died. His wish was granted but, like Knox, he was moved when new buildings were put up. He did have a street named after him though – Marlin's Wynd.

8 True ... probably. The Earl was a giant of a young man but was mentally ill. His family kept him locked in a room in Queensberry House in Canongate but his father went out one day and the Earl broke out. He followed his nose to the kitchen, where a kitchen boy was turning a piece of roast meat over the fire. When the father came home the meat was gone – and the kitchen boy was roasting over the fire instead. He had been half eaten.

9 True ... possibly. That's what the legend says. Around 1800 a gang dug up a grave, then opened the coffin to steal the body and sell it. They noticed the woman's hands were covered in rings and thought the quickest way to get them

was to cut off her fingers. But as soon as they started cutting she screamed and sat up.

Many doctors in the 1800s were not very bright and couldn't spot when a patient was in a deep sleep. They just said, 'Dead – bury them.' They say some people must have been buried alive.

10 False ... but only just. Charles Dickens wrote *A Christmas Carol* after seeing a gravestone in Edinburgh. On it was carved the name 'Ebenezer Scroggie' and underneath was his job: 'Meal man' – he sold 'meal' to make porridge. But Charlie Dickens must have left his glasses at home. He THOUGHT the gravestone said 'Mean man'. Imagine being buried with 'Mean man' on your grave.

HOLYROOD HORRORS

Holyroodhouse is a fine building just 1.6 km from Edinburgh Castle. But even a pleasant place can have a putrid past…

Rotten for Rizzio

Mary Queen of Scots was married to Lord Darnley, who was a dangerous man. They were living in the Palace of Holyroodhouse when Darnley fell into a filthy mood. He had two problems…

• He was married to the Queen but had not been crowned king and he thought he should be.

• He decided he was jealous of the Queen's musician and secretary, David Rizzio, a harmless little man.

On 9 March 1566 Darnley set about a vicious plot. One of the most powerful plotters was Lord Ruthven. Ruthven told his story to Queen Elizabeth I of England as he lay dying in Newcastle. Here is his story…

FOR MANY DAYS LORD DARNLEY HAD BEEN SAYING TO ME…

I CAN'T STAND RIZZIO ANY LONGER. IF HE'S NOT DEAD SOON THEN I'LL KILL HIM WITH MY OWN HANDS!

HE GOT ME TO GATHER A GROUP OF LORDS TOGETHER AND PLOTTED TO KILL RIZZIO AT HOLYROODHOUSE

ON THE EVENING OF 9 MARCH WE BURST INTO THE ROOM WHERE MARY WAS HAVING SUPPER WITH RIZZIO AND HER FRIEND BOTHWELL...

AND KILL THAT BOTHWELL WHILE YOU ARE AT IT!

TAKE HIM OUT AND KILL HIM

BOTHWELL ESCAPED THROUGH A WINDOW. RIZZIO HID BEHIND THE QUEEN'S SKIRTS

DON'T LET THEM TAKE ME, YOUR MAJESTY!

I TORE HIM AWAY FROM THE QUEEN AND TOOK HIM TO ANOTHER ROOM. I ORDERED THE LORDS TO KILL HIM

THEY TELL ME THEY FOUND 56 STAB WOUNDS ON THE CORPSE!

You have to wonder if little David had one last chance to sing before he died…

SILENT NIGHT,
HOLEY NIGHT,
GOT HOLES IN
ME BODY AND
HOLES IN ME
TIGHTS!

Mary never forgave dreadful Darnley. You may be pleased to know that he didn't last long after Rizzio's murder.

Deadly for Darnley

Mary wept when Rizzio was dragged away. When she finally heard that he was dead, she stopped crying and said…

No more tears now. I will think upon revenge.

On 1 February 1567 Darnley felt poorly – though not as poorly as Rizzio felt after being stabbed 56 times. Mary took hubby Darnley to a house called Kirk O'Fields near the city walls. 'You need peace and rest,' she said. Mary promised to stay and look after him, but on the night of 9 February she slipped out to a wedding party.

Did Darnley enjoy the peace? Not after Mary's friend Bothwell planted a bomb in the house. Darnley staggered out into the garden, where his enemies stabbed and strangled him. David Rizzio was avenged and Mary married Bothwell.

Happy ending? Of course not. Mary was accused of her husband's murder and driven out of Scotland. She fled to England and asked her cousin Queen Elizabeth I to give her shelter. Elizabeth 'sheltered' Mary in castle prisons for 19 years – then had her head lopped off.

Kidnapping a king

Holyrood was a fine palace but a poor castle. On 27 December 1591 the Earl of Bothwell broke into Holyroodhouse without a hitch – his gang of 50 men slipped in through a stable door and stole the keys.

Bothwell's plan was to kidnap Mary's son, who was now King James VI, and murder his minister, Maitland. The Earl had a band of soldiers to help him.

JAMES COULDN'T AFFORD AN ARMY OR EVEN A BODYGUARD. I SIMPLY WALKED INTO JAMES' PALACE TO TAKE HIM

I FLED TO A TOWER AND LOCKED BOTHWELL OUT

MY GANG SET FIRE TO THE DOOR AND TRIED TO BREAK IT DOWN WITH HAMMERS

LUCKILY A GROUP OF PEOPLE FROM EDINBURGH TOWN RUSHED TO MY AID AND DROVE BOTHWELL OFF

HE OFFERED A REWARD FOR ANYONE WHO WOULD KILL ME! SO TWO YEARS LATER I WAS BACK AT HOLYROOD...

THIS TIME I RAN TO THE QUEEN'S BEDROOM CRYING 'TREASON!'

What happened next?

a) James killed him with a single thrust to the heart.

b) James didn't have the nerve to kill him.

c) James took the sword but cut his own finger and ran to get a doctor.

Nasty Nichol

David Rizzio wasn't the only person to meet a blood-soaked death at Holyrood. In 1720 a drunken gambler called Nichol Mushat grew to hate his wife and decided to get rid of her...

- He spread lies about how wicked she was, hoping to get a divorce. That didn't work.
- He tried to poison her with huge amounts of deadly medicine. She was a tough lady – the poison didn't work.
- He took her to King's Park near Holyrood one winter night and cut her throat till her head almost dropped off. That worked.

NOBODY'S **THAT** TOUGH!

Nasty Nichol was caught and executed. A pile of stones, called a 'cairn', was left to mark the spot where the murder happened.

CRUEL CRIMINALS

Every city has its criminals. But some of Edinburgh's were as cruel and cunning as you'd ever wish to meet.

The Brodie mysteries

There have been many evil Edinburgh people – but William Brodie was one of the strangest. He was a mystery right to the end … and even PAST the end!

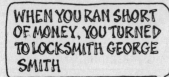
WHEN YOU RAN SHORT OF MONEY, YOU TURNED TO LOCKSMITH GEORGE SMITH

THE DEACON WORKED IN PEOPLE'S HOMES MAKING CABINETS. HE BORROWED THE KEYS AND I COPIED THEM

AT NIGHT YOU WENT BACK AND ROBBED THEM

CHUCKLE!

NO ONE KNEW HOW WE DID IT. IT WAS A MYSTERY

CLICK!

THIS IS YOUR GREAT INVENTION- THE SCAFFOLD WITH A TRAP- DOOR TO MAKE HANGING QUICK AND EASY

I WAS PROUD OF THAT!

BUT WHEN ONE OF YOUR GANG BETRAYED YOU, YOU WERE HANGED ON YOUR OWN MACHINE!

OR WAS I? IT WAS ANOTHER MYSTERY!

Deft theft

So how did a top Edinburgh gent have a secret life as a burglar?

1 He robbed houses while rich people were in church on a Sunday. One old lady was too ill to go to church but he slipped into her house anyway, wearing a mask over his mouth. He stole money from her cabinet then bowed to her as he left. The old lady said to herself...

Surely that was Deacon Brodie!

But she didn't believe her own eyes so she didn't tell anyone.

2 Brodie's gang locked up after they had robbed a shop or house, so no one knew when the money had disappeared. Most thieves just smashed a door.

3 Brodie always knew the place he was going to rob and where to find the money. Sometimes the target was a house where he had made cabinets. But when he earmarked the city tax office he made several visits and saw where the key was kept. He made a copy using window putty.

4 Brodie didn't just steal money. He stole hundreds of kilos of tea from a grocer, gold ornaments from a library and silk from a shop in the High Street.

5 Brodie was betrayed by one of his own gang after the tax office burglary. He escaped to Holland but wrote letters to friends back in Edinburgh. The letters gave away his hiding place and he was caught.

Crafty collar

But what is the mystery about his hanging? According to legend, Brodie survived. There are three different stories…

1 He stepped on the scaffold but the rope was too short – a short drop would not have killed him. It took three tries to get the rope long enough. Was that part of his escape plan? Did he pay the hangman to give him a chance? Friends could have cut him down before he was quite dead.

2 Brodie wore a clever steel collar round his neck. When he dropped, the collar would stop him from choking and his friends could rescue him.

3 Brodie swallowed a pipe that stayed in his throat. Like the collar, it would stop his neck being crushed by the hangman's rope.

The truth? Brodie was hanged at the Tolbooth, just a few metres from the Lawnmarket where he was born. His body WAS taken away by friends and no one knows where they dug his grave. So there is just a chance one of these stories could be true.

Mystery murder

Edinburgh has had some pretty bizarre murders throughout its history. Here is one true tale to terrify your teacher with.

James Robb's robbery

In 1862 Robb was robbed near Edinburgh (which serves him right for having a name like that). An Irish man called McCarty smacked his head with a hammer and stole his watch. McCarty then went to America where, 20 years later, he joined the army. While he was chatting to a Scot called Matthew Gray he told the story of the robbery. He was amazed when Gray said...

McCarty was arrested but escaped into the wilds of America. He was killed by Native American warriors. They do say 'Set a thief to catch a thief,' but *Horrible Histories* says...

Bodies for sale

Of all the horrors of Edinburgh the gruesome twosome William Burke and William Hare are the most horrible. Here is their savage story...

Oh, but William Burke is a smooth talker. He's been the servant to a priest in Ireland ... bless him. He arrives in Edinburgh and meets up with William Hare. They love their drink and with their wives they make two rowdy couples. Burke and Hare. Hare and Burke. Names that will shame Edinburgh's name for ever.

An old man called Donald rents a room from William Hare in Tanner's Close in the Old Town. The place is a slum. A stinking straw bed in a stinking pit of a house. On 27 November 1827, Hare knocks at the door. 'Have you my rent today, Mr Donald?' he asks. No reply. He knocks louder. No reply. There never will be. Donald is dead.

'Dead?' Mrs Hare cries. 'He can't be dead! He owes us four pounds.'

'Dead,' their friend William Burke chuckles. 'That's good.'

'He owes us four pounds! We'll never get it now.'

'Oh, yes you will,' Burke breathes. 'The doctors at the hospital want nice fresh bodies. They need them to cut up and examine.'

'What for?' Mrs Hare shudders.

'To find out how our bodies work. To teach young doctors. To help to make us living folk get better.'

'They'll take the body and save us all the cost of a funeral?' Hare asks happily.'

'Better. They'll pay us – at least five pounds. Wrap old Donald in a sack. I'll fetch a barrow from the back.'

Seven pounds and ten shillings they make. Seven pounds and ten shillings they spend on drink. Then their purses and their throats run dry. No more cold corpses to sell – not yet. Not till Burke meets a drunken old woman in the street. Oh, but William Burke is a smooth talker...

'You look cold, my dear. Can't afford a bed for the night? We have a spare one over in Tanner's Close. Come with me. We'll see to you, Grandma. All your troubles will be over. Just turn in here ... then through this door. You have no friends? Poor love. No one to miss you when you're gone? Ah, home at last. This is my friend William Hare. Just rest here on this warm straw. We laid it fresh last month. Lie down... Now Will Hare, close her lips and nip her nose so she can't breathe. I'll lie across her chest and squeeze the last air from her lungs. That's right. That's good. She's still and not a mark left on her. Pass that sack, my friend!'

And when the cash is gone they start again. And again.

Seventeen helpless people end up on the doctor's slab. A year goes by and then, at last, the neighbours call the law. Margery Campbell's corpse is found.

'Who killed her?' the police ask.

Burke looks at Hare. Hare looks at Burke. Hare points at Burke. 'It was him,' he says. 'Burke's the murderer.'

Burke shakes his head – a head that's headed for the hangman's noose. His smooth talk won't talk him out of trouble now. It's over. Burke is hanged ... and Hare goes free.

Did you know…?

1 Burke's body was sent to the doctors for cutting up after he was hanged. Seems fair enough.

2 Burke's skeleton was preserved and is still on show today in the Edinburgh University Anatomy Museum. A pocket book was also made of his skin and that is on display at the Police Museum on Royal Mile. Nice.

3 Burke's corpse was viewed by 30,000 people. Some of the posh Edinburgh folk even managed to get pieces of his pickled skin to keep. The sliced skin must have looked good on the posh people's mantelpiece.

4 Hare changed his name, went free and got a job in a lime factory. But his workmates found out who he really was and threw him in the lime, which blinded him. He ended his miserable life as a blind beggar.

I FEELA RIGHT LEMON!

5 Burke and Hare made a sticky plaster from tar. They held it over the victim's mouth and nose till they were dead. Some say they killed as many as 30 victims this way. Their tar-plaster murder method was known as 'burking'.

6 The Edinburgh doctors were *allowed* to cut up dead criminals. The trouble was, there weren't enough of them so they bought bodies to experiment on, even though it was against the law. Any body of anybody was better than no body.

7 The surgeon Dr Robert Knox paid the killers for the bodies. He must have known they were murder victims but he said nothing. He was never punished.

8 Doctor Knox turned his body-cutting into a show for the students. He practised just as actors do for a play and gave his show dressed in fine clothes and jewellery. The corpses must have thought it really fine.

9 Bodysnatchers dug up fresh graves to steal bodies for doctors like Knox. People started having their dead friends buried under iron cages to keep the bodysnatchers out. One snatcher called Merrylees even sold his own sister. You wouldn't do that, would you?

10 Burke and Hare are remembered as the world's most famous bodysnatchers … yet they never snatched a single body! They were simple murderers. How odd is that?

NO SMOKE WITHOUT FIRE

There were lots of fires in the rickety old tenements (town houses) of Edinburgh.

Then, on 15 November 1824, Edinburgh had its own Great Fire.

Here are a few foul facts you probably didn't know about the 1824 Great Fire…

1 There had been a pretty big fire on 24 June – a sort of 'Not-So-Great Fire' of Edinburgh – months before the Great Fire. The ruined houses hadn't even been cleared away. Did they learn from the Not-So-Great Fire of Edinburgh?

DON'T BE DAFT — OF COURSE WE DIDN'T!

2 The Great Fire started in a printing company on the High Street. The firemen soon gave up trying to put it out. They tried to save the houses nearby instead. But the narrow streets called 'closes' were like a maze – and the firemen couldn't get close. It was midnight and they were stumbling around in the dark alleys – except when they caught fire.

RED SKY AT NIGHT MEANS ME HAIR IS ALIGHT!

3 The fire was almost out by the next morning … but a breeze blew sparks on to the Tron Kirk (Church) and it burst into flames. The lead on the roof melted and splashed on to the firemen.

YOU CAN DRAG A HOSE TO WATER BUT A ROOF IT MUST BE LEAD

4 No sooner was that blaze out than another fire broke out in a high tenement on the other side of Parliament Square. The firemen didn't have ladders long enough to reach the top. After a day and a half the fire was almost out. House walls were about to fall down so soldiers blew them up. Six people died in the Great Fire of London – Edinburgh's fire killed at least eight and maybe thirteen.

5 Edinburgh Council decided it needed a better fire service so it gave the job to James Braidwood. It was the best fire service in the world … till Braidwood got a better job running the London Fire Service.

6 In 1861 a fire broke out near London Bridge. Braidwood rushed to take charge. But a wall fell on him and crushed him to death.

Did you know…?

Waverley railway station in Edinburgh is built on land that used to be a swamp. People tipped their rubbish into it and it stank. In 1765 the council decided to dry it out and build a bridge across, but a heavy rainstorm washed away some of the rubbish holding up the bridge and it fell down, killing five people.

SCRUTINIZE A SCOT

First find someone from Scotland. Then ask if they know much about Edinburgh. If they are daft enough to say 'Yes' then ask them these ten torturing questions...

1 In the 1650s John Nicholl wrote: 'At this time there was brought to the nation a wonderful thing called ... It was kept in Canongate and you had to pay three pence to see it.' What was it?
a) Excalibur – King Arthur's sword
b) A two-headed man
c) A camel

2 In the 1700s the law said women could not wear them on their heads. What?
a) Hats
b) Shawls
c) Knickers

3 In 1865 the Theatre Royal caught fire. The stage manager called the fireman for help. But the fireman didn't come. Why not?
a) He was deaf.
b) He was dead.
c) He thought it was a joke.

4 John Chiesly shot a judge and was hanged in Edinburgh's Grassmarket. His body was stolen from the scaffold and found years later. How did they know it was John Chiesly?

a) He was hanged with the murder pistol round his neck – it was still on the corpse.

b) He was in a coffin and a label on the coffin said, 'John Chiesly'.

c) A ghost leapt out and said, 'I am John Chiesly and you will be cursed if you bother my bones.'

5 In 1785 the famous Italian balloonist Lunardi took off from Edinburgh to fly across the Firth of Forth. He landed near Ceres in Fife. The people of Ceres were a bit upset when he landed. Why?

a) He landed on the church and wrecked the roof.

b) He turned out to be a human. They thought he was an angel.

c) He refused to give the Ceres children a ride.

6 Major Weir was potty about praying. Then, in 1670, at the age of 76 he became simply potty and said he was a witch. What did the people of Edinburgh do to him?

a) They gave him a hot cup of tea (with whisky) and cared for him till he felt better.

b) They chained him to a wall in the Tolbooth Prison and hoped he'd get better.

c) They had him strangled and burned as a witch.

7 Sir Walter Scott held a party to welcome King George IV to Edinburgh in 1822. King George gave his drinking glass to Sir Walter as a present. What happened to the glass?
a) Sir Walter gave it away saying, 'I already have a pair of glasses.'
b) Sir Walter used it to feed milk to his pet cat.
c) Sir Walter sat on it and sliced his backside.

8 Greyfriars cemetery was famous for bodysnatchers who dug up the bodies and sold them to doctors. When was the last case of a body being dug up?
a) April 2004
b) November 1904
c) June 1804

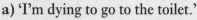

9 In 1861 young James McIver lived in some ramshackle flats called Paisley Close. On 24 November that year they fell down and buried James. What did he shout to the men rescuing him?
a) 'I'm dying to go to the toilet.'
b) 'I'm going to die in a minute if you don't get that pig off my head.'
c) 'I'm not dead yet.'

10 In Canongate in 1867 a man was making fireworks. A spark started a fire and the building burst into flames. One man called Ballantyne was a truly great hero. What was brilliantly brave Ballantyne's job?

a) A children's author (of course)

b) A teacher (rescuing kids? Unlikely)

c) An out-of-work Father Christmas (got in before the fire could sleigh everyone)

Answers:

1c) A camel was a rare sight in Edinburgh. To keep it company the camel had a little baboon.

2b) The punishment for wearing a shawl over your head was a fine of £5 AND the shawl was taken off you. Do it a third time and you were banished from Edinburgh!

3c) The workers in the theatre often shouted 'Fire!' just to annoy Fireman Syme. This time Syme ignored the cries that were for real. The theatre burned to the ground and six people died. It was Friday the thirteenth. Creepy, eh? A new theatre was built on the spot in 1866. It burned down in

1875. A new theatre was built on the spot in 1876. (No, that is not an echo.) It burned down in 1884. A new theatre was built on the spot. It also burned down … but not until 1946. This time a new theatre was NOT built on the unlucky spot. Wise move.

4a) First the executioner chopped off the Chiesly hand that had pulled the trigger. Then Chiesly was hanged with the pistol around his neck. His body should have been taken away to the hospital to be cut up by the surgeons. But criminals hated the thought of being chopped to pieces after death – they thought they'd get to heaven in bits! So Chiesly's friends stole his corpse and buried it under the floor of a house in Dalry Park. In 1965 it was found – with the pistol still round Chiesly's neck. The hand was missing though – his friends didn't manage to pinch that.

5b) The people of Ceres had never seen a balloon before so when it drifted towards them they started praying to it. They were sure it was the Angel Gabriel.

6c) Major Weir was a war hero and mad about religion. He went around Edinburgh praying and always had a black stick with him – a stick carved with strange faces. He lived with his sister Grizel in a building called the Bow just off the Grassmarket. (It was knocked down in 1830 because it was haunted.)

When he became mentally ill he told people he was a witch. At first they didn't believe him. Then law officers looked in his room and found money wrapped up in rags. One officer took the money and threw the rag on the fire. The rag shot up the chimney and exploded. Spooky! Then Grizel Weir said it was all true and that she was a witch as well! The Fairy Queen had taught her how to spin wool and a devil took her for rides in a fiery coach.

The major was strangled and burned by the road to Leith. The next day his sister suffered the same horrible end in the Grassmarket. His black stick was thrown into the flames.

7c) Sir Walter tucked the glass into a coat pocket and took it home. But a friend was waiting to say hello and Sir Walt forgot about the glass. It slipped through a hole in the pocket and ended up in his coat tail. When he sat down he crushed the glass. He screamed. His wife thought he'd sat on a pair of scissors!

8a) That's right, 2004. Two young Scots kicked in the door to the tomb of the judge Sir George Mackenzie. They then found his coffin with a mummified body. One of the youths hacked off the head. They were caught and faced a jail sentence of 20 years. In fact they got off with 'community service'. They had to work without pay to keep parts of Edinburgh tidy. Which parts? The graveyards, of course.

9c) When the fire brigade arrived they saw James McIver's foot sticking out of the rubble. As they sawed the beam off him brave little James cried out, 'Heave away, lads, I'm not dead yet.' He lived. There is now a carving in the wall of the new Paisley Close showing a picture of James with his famous words. But 35 others weren't so lucky – they were crushed when the 25-metre building fell down because the wood pillars had rotted away.

10a) Obvious really. Anyone who writes books for children is a hero. R. M. Ballantyne's best-seller was an adventure story called *The Coral Island*. He was given a medal for rushing through the smoke-filled house to find the body of a little girl.

Never mind – he was a hero for trying! All children's authors should be given gold medals and a lifetime supply of deep-fried Mars bars because we are all heroes.

EPILOGUE

There is a hill to the east of Edinburgh called Arthur's Seat.
In 1836 five boys were hunting rabbits on the hillside when
their dog uncovered 17 tiny coffins with 17 tiny dolls inside.
No one knows why they were put there. Some people believe
it may have been in memory of Burke and Hare's 17 victims.

So now you know what to say when a visitor asks you…

And that has to be the end of this history of Edinburgh,
because the jokes can't get any worse.